WITHDRAWN

Comparing Bugs

Bug
Food

Charlotte Guillain

Heinemann Library
Chicago, Illinois

Edited by Rebecca Rissman and Catherine Veitch
Designed by Joanna Hinton-Malivoire
Picture research by Elizabeth Alexander
Production by Duncan Gilbert and Victoria Fitzgerald
Originated by Heinemann Library
Printed and bound in China by South China Printing
Company Ltd

14 13 12 11 10
10 9 8 7 6 5 4 3 2 1

Library of Congress Cataloging-in-Publication Data
Bug food / Charlotte Guillain. -- 1st ed.
    p. cm. -- (Comparing bugs)
ISBN 978-1-4329-3569-6 (hc) -- ISBN 978-1-4329-3578-8 (pb)
QL467.2.C856 2010
595.7153--dc22
                                                    2009025552

www.heinemannraintree.com
Visit our website to find out
more information about
Heinemann-Raintree books.

To order:

☎ Phone 888-454-2279

🖥 Visit www.heinemannraintree.com
    to browse our catalog and order online.

Acknowledgments
The author and publishers are grateful to the following for permission
to reproduce copyright material: Alamy pp. **4** (© Roger Eritja), **15** (©
blickwinkel), **17** (© blickwinkel), **16** (© B. Mete Uz); Ardea.com pp. **13** (©
John Daniels), **18** (© Pascal Goetgheluck); Corbis pp. **9** (© Steffen Schmidt/
epa), **23 bottom** (© Steffen Schmidt/epa); FLPA p. **19** (© Heidi & Hans-
Juergen Koch); Getty Images p. **8** (© George Grall/National Geographic);
iStockphoto pp. **5** (© andrey Pavlov), **6** (© Michal Boubin), **11** (© Robert
Kobsa), **22 top right**; NHPA p. **20** (A.N.T. Photo Library); Photolibrary pp.
7 (Patti Murray/Animals Animals); RSPCA p. **19** (Tim Martin); Shutterstock
pp. **10** (© Cathleen Clapper), **12** (© Kletr), **14** (© Johan Swanepoel), **22
top left** (© alle), **22 bottom left** (© alle), **22 bottom right** (© Eric
Isselée), **23 top** (© Yellowj).

Cover photograph of a caterpillar (European Swallowtail) feeding on carrot
leaves reproduced with permission of Ardea (© Steve Hopkin). Back cover
photograph of beetles rolling a ball of dung in South Africa reproduced with
permission of Shutterstock (© Johan Swanepoel).

The publishers would like to thank Nancy Harris and Kate Wilson for their
assistance in the preparation of this book.

Every effort has been made to contact copyright holders of any material
reproduced in this book. Any omissions will be rectified in subsequent
printings if notice is given to the publisher.

Contents

Meet the Bugs 4

Plants 6

Blood and Poo. 12

Eating Other Animals 16

How Big? 22

Picture Glossary. 23

Index 24

Meet the Bugs

There are many different types of bugs.

Bugs eat many different foods.

Most bugs get their food from plants.

leaves

Most caterpillars eat leaves.

dead wood

Wood lice eat dead wood.

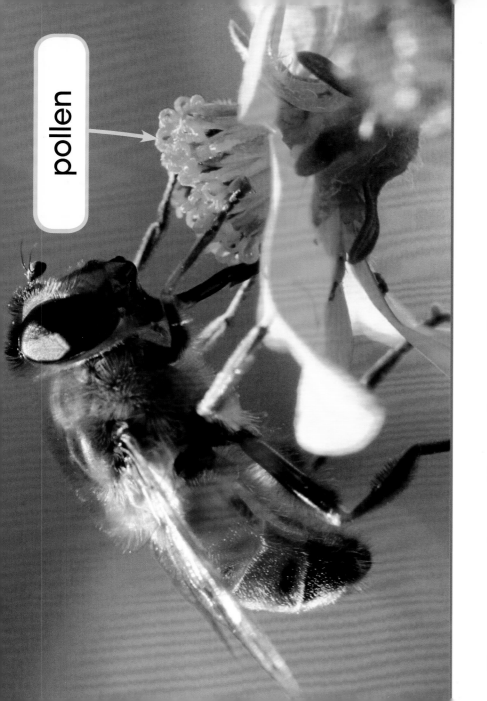

pollen

Bees eat pollen from flowers.

Milkweed bugs eat seeds.

seed

fruit

Some wasps eat fruit.

Blood and Poo

Some mosquitoes suck blood from animals. Then they fly away.

Ticks suck blood from animals.
Then they drop off.

Dung beetles eat poo.

poo

poo

Many flies eat poo, too.

Eating Other Animals

grasshopper

Some wasps eat other insects.

blackfly

Ladybugs eat blackflies.

A praying mantis might eat another praying mantis.

Some spiders eat other spiders.

Some bugs eat larger animals.

Some big centipedes eat mice.

How Big?

beetle

caterpillar

earwig

spider

Look at how big some of the bugs in this book can be.

Picture Glossary

insect very small creature with six legs

pollen golden powder inside flowers

Index

blood 12, 13

fruit 11

leaves 7

plants 6

pollen 9, 23

poo 14, 15

seed 10

wood 8

Notes to Parents and Teachers

Before reading

Make a list of bugs with the children. Try to include insects, arachnids (e.g. spiders), crustaceans (e.g. wood lice), myriapods (e.g. centipedes and millipedes), and earthworms. Do they know what each bug eats? Ask them to make suggestions if they do not know and then read the book to see if they guessed correctly.

After reading

- Did the children find out what all the bugs on their list eat? If they are still not sure about any of them, use reference books or the Internet together to find the answers.
- If you have a garden in the school grounds, look at the growing plants between spring and late summer and see if any bugs are eating them. Are there any bees or butterflies visiting the flowers? Look for pollen on bees' legs and bodies. You can also look for signs that a bug has been feeding on a particular plant.
- Start a class wormery to observe what compost worms eat. Discuss how these worms help us to recycle waste and help the environment.